Key Stage One Mathematics

Set A
Paper 1: Arithmetic

First name	
Middle name	
Last name	

For this test you are allowed to use:

a **pen** or a **pencil**   a **rubber**   and a **ruler**.

Total marks

Exam Set MHEP13

1 6 + 7 = ☐

2 16 − 5 = ☐

3 13 + 6 = ☐

4. 20 − ☐ = 8

1 mark

5. 45 − 10 = ☐

1 mark

6. 2 × 6 = ☐

1 mark

7 6 + 3 + 2 = ☐

8 4 × 5 = ☐

9 30 + ☐ = 90

10 $10 \times 2 =$ ☐

1 mark

11 $16 \div 2 =$ ☐

1 mark

12 $78 - 10 - 10 =$ ☐

1 mark

13 $30 \div 5 = $ ☐

14 $34 - 27 = $ ☐

15 $19 + 20 = $ ☐

16 $\frac{1}{2}$ of 14 = ☐

1 mark

17 12 + 48 = ☐

1 mark

18. 10 × 10 =

19. 5 × 3 =

20 $\frac{1}{4}$ of 16 = ☐

1 mark

21 24 + 49 = ☐

1 mark

22 43 − 18 =

23 60 ÷ 5 =

24 46 + ☐ = 81

25 $\frac{3}{4}$ of 12 = ☐

END OF TEST

[Blank Page]

Key Stage One Mathematics

Set A
Paper 2: Reasoning

First name	
Middle name	
Last name	

For this test you are allowed to use:
a **pen** or a **pencil**   a **rubber**   and a **ruler**.

Total marks

1

1 mark

2

1 mark

3

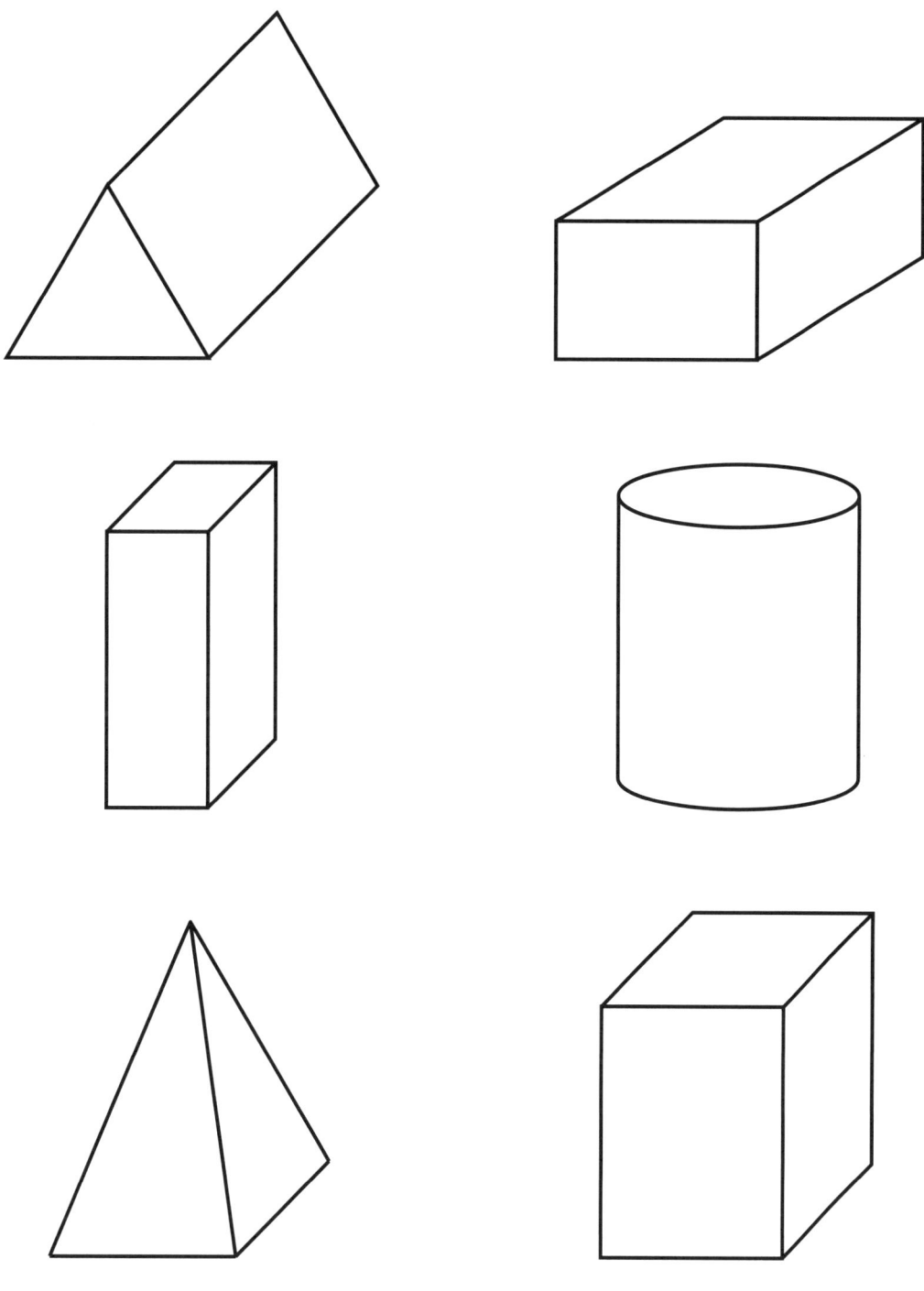

1 mark

4

[   ]

1 mark

5

[oranges]

1 mark

6 Put a ring around the **heaviest** object.

1 mark

7 Write **+** or **−** in each box to make these sums correct.

20 ☐ 13 = 7

20 = 7 ☐ 13

1 mark

8 Daniel draws this shape.

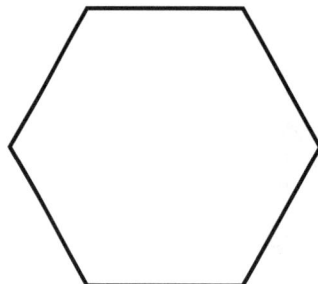

Circle the name of the shape he has drawn.

Pentagon   Hexagon   Octagon

1 mark

9 Look at this cube.

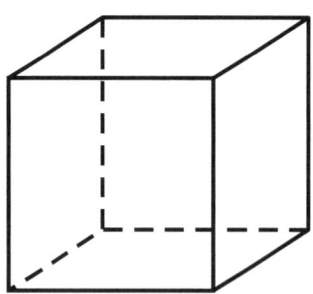

How many **faces** does it have?

faces

1 mark

10 Circle **three** numbers below that add up to **100**.

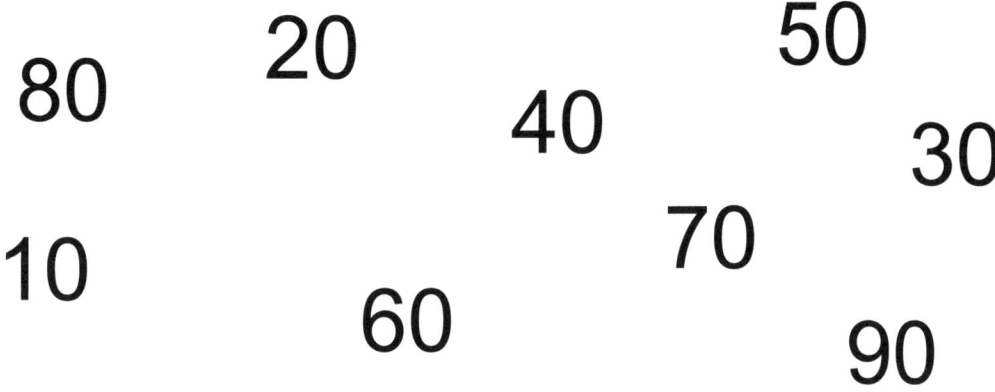

1 mark

11

Colin sells **12** chocolate ice creams and **13** strawberry ice creams.

How many ice creams does Colin sell in total?

ice creams

1 mark

12 Look at this number line.

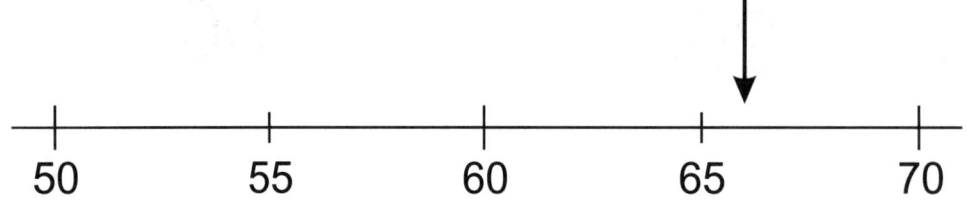

What number is the arrow pointing to?

1 mark

13 Poppy and Daniel have **25** toy cars between them.
Poppy has **11** toy cars.

How many toy cars does Daniel have?

toy cars

1 mark

14 Poppy makes **10** cupcakes.

She puts **4** chocolate buttons on each cupcake.
How many chocolate buttons does she use?

chocolate buttons

1 mark

She packs all **10** cupcakes into boxes.
She puts **2** cupcakes in each box.

How many boxes does she use?

boxes

1 mark

15 Draw the line of symmetry on this shape.

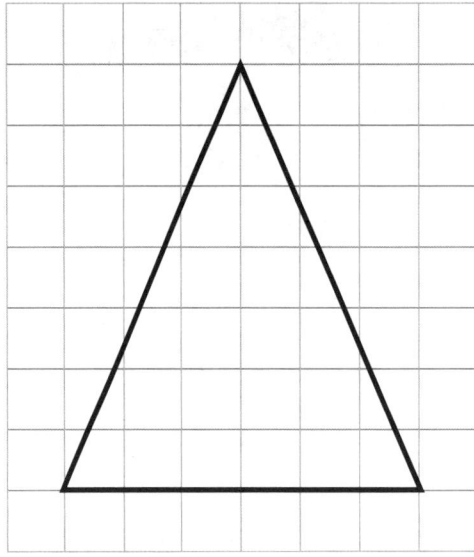

16 Match each temperature to the right thermometer.

14 °C   13 °C   11 °C

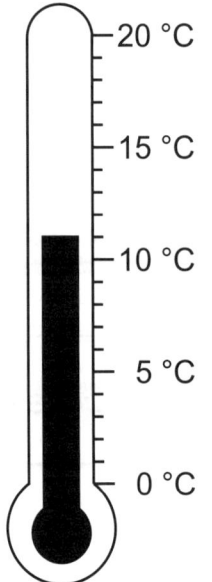 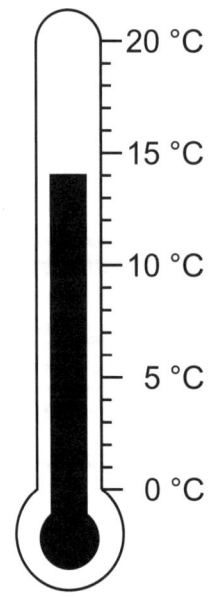 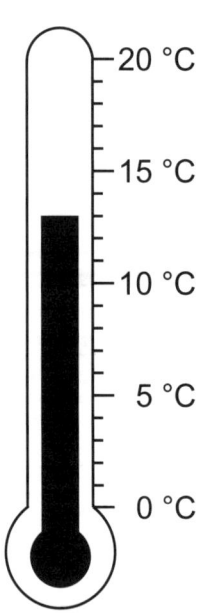

17 The chart shows how many sunny days there were in France, Italy, Spain and the UK last week.

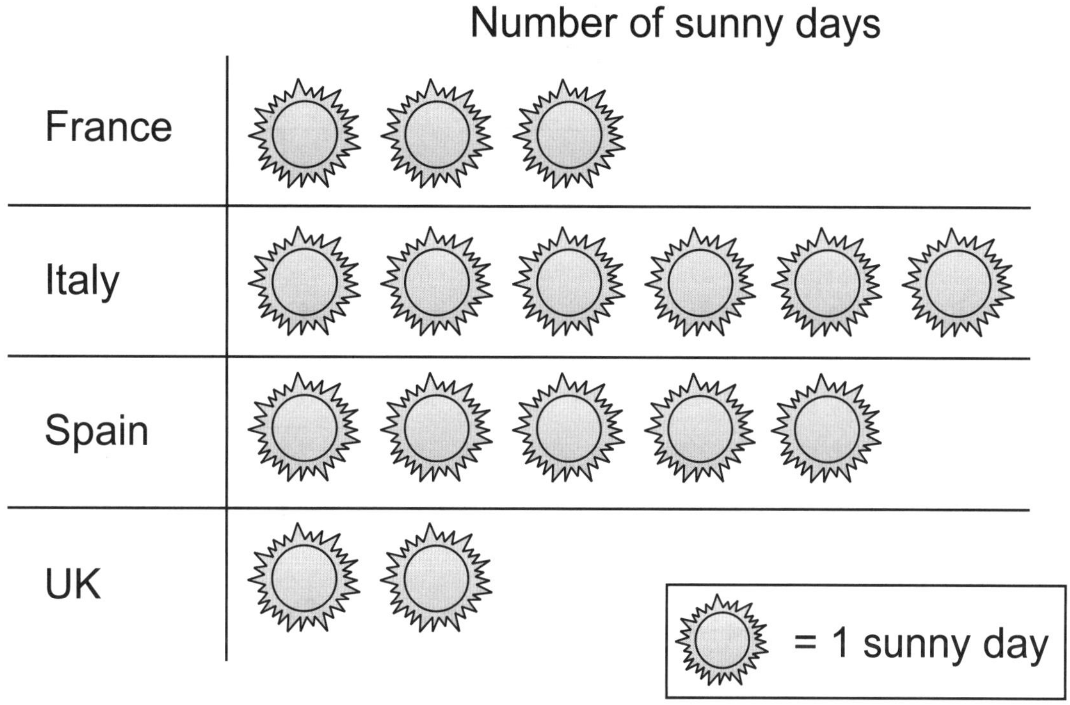

Number of sunny days

France	☀ ☀ ☀
Italy	☀ ☀ ☀ ☀ ☀ ☀
Spain	☀ ☀ ☀ ☀ ☀
UK	☀ ☀

☀ = 1 sunny day

Which country had the **most** sunny days?

1 mark

How many **more** sunny days were there in Spain than in France?

1 mark

18 Fill in the two missing numbers in this sequence.

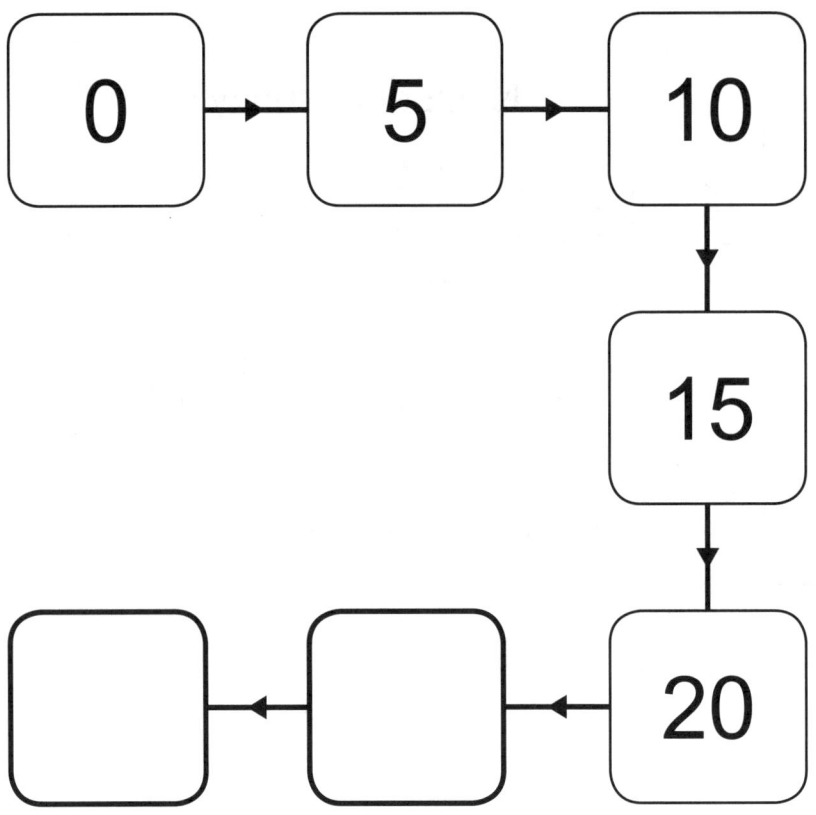

19 Shade $\frac{1}{2}$ of this shape.

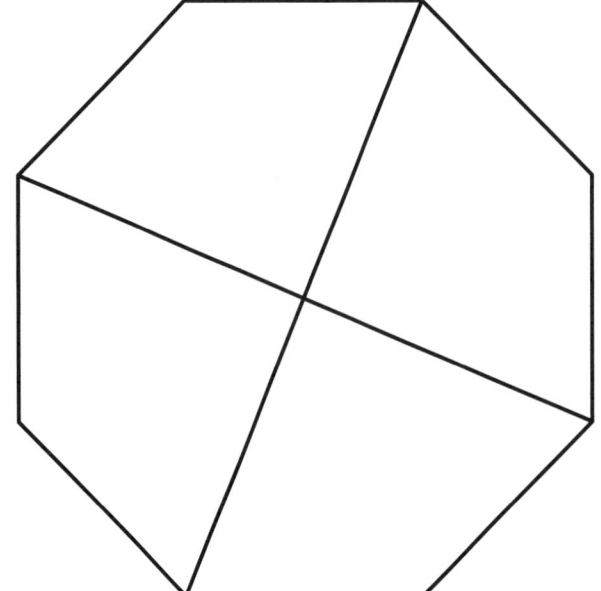

20 Billy has **23** building bricks.

Janet has **44** building bricks.

How many building bricks do they have altogether?

1 mark

21 Put a ring around the clock that shows the time '**ten to four**'.

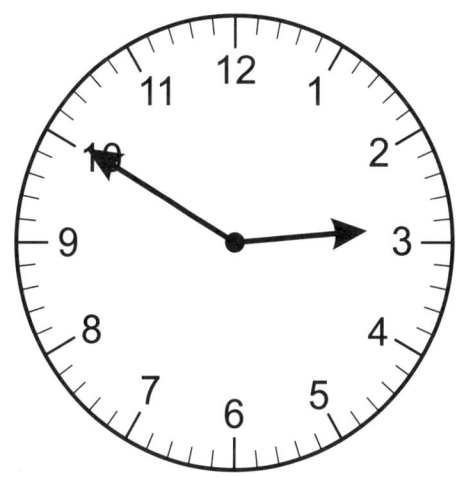

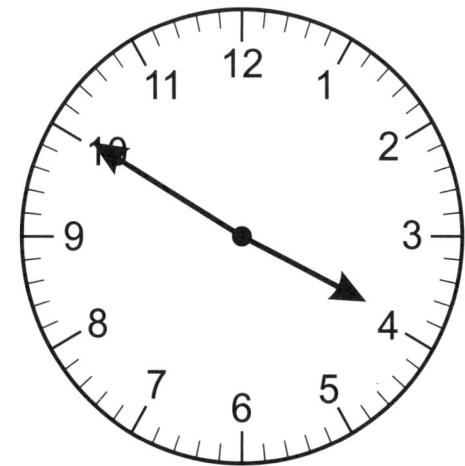

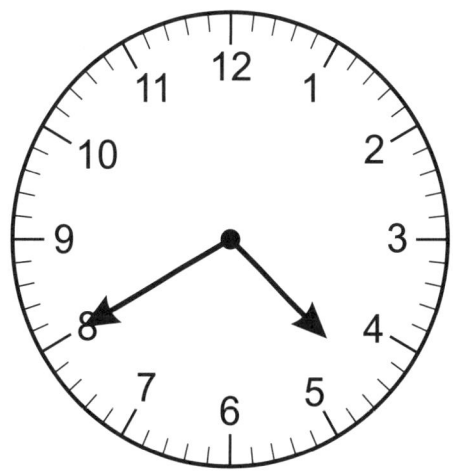

1 mark

22 Daniel has **15** pencils.

He gives $\frac{1}{3}$ of his pencils to Poppy.

How many pencils does he give to Poppy?

pencils

23 Look at these numbers.

27   35

Write each number in the correct box.

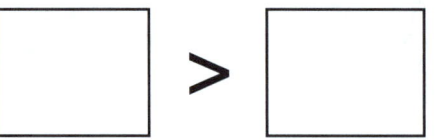

24 Poppy has these coins in her purse.

A key ring costs **95p**.
Does Poppy have enough money to buy a key ring?
Write 'Yes' or 'No' in the box.

25 Look at these calculations.

$$4 + 7 \quad 4 - 8 \quad 8 - 4 \quad 7 + 4$$

Put a ring around the **two** calculations that give the same answer.

Now look at these calculations.

$$3 \div 9 \quad 3 \times 6 \quad 9 \div 3 \quad 6 \times 3$$

Put a ring around the **two** calculations that give the same answer.

26 Poppy did a Maths test at **2** o'clock on Monday **afternoon**.

Daniel did a Maths test at **10** o'clock on Monday **morning**.

Put a ring around the correct word in the sentence below.

Poppy did her Maths test **before / after** Daniel.

1 mark

27 Poppy collects **5** pebbles every day.

How many days will it take her to collect **45** pebbles?

days

1 mark

28 Daniel has **£60**.

He buys a coat and a t-shirt.

Item	Price
Coat	£12
Dress	£9
T-shirt	£10
Hat	£3

How much money does he have left?

Show your working.

£

2 marks

29 Here is a rectangle.

It is rotated a **quarter turn anti-clockwise**.

Put a tick (✔) next to the picture that shows the rectangle after it has been rotated.

1 mark

30 To balance the scales, there needs to be the same weight on each side.

Daniel puts **four 3 kg** weights on one side of the scales.

Poppy puts **six 2 kg** weights on the other side of the scales. Do the scales balance? Write 'Yes' or 'No' in the box.

Show your working.

2 marks

END OF TEST

[Blank Page]

Key Stage One Mathematics

Set B
Paper 1: Arithmetic

First name	
Middle name	
Last name	

For this test you are allowed to use:

a **pen** or a **pencil**   a **rubber**   and a **ruler**.

Total marks

Exam Set MHEP13

1 $9 - 7 =$ ☐

1 mark

2 $20 + 9 =$ ☐

1 mark

3 $37 + 10 =$ ☐

1 mark

4 $7 \times 2 = \boxed{}$

1 mark

5 $48 - 6 = \boxed{}$

1 mark

6 $8 - \boxed{} = 5$

1 mark

7 18 + 20 = ☐

1 mark

8 4 × 10 = ☐

1 mark

9 9 + 5 + 3 = ☐

1 mark

10. 17 + 4 = ☐

11. ☐ × 10 = 90

12. ☐ − 20 = 60

13 $7 \times 5 = \square$

1 mark

14 $56 - 9 = \square$

1 mark

15 $50 \div 5 = \square$

1 mark

16 20 + 30 + 30 = ☐

17 37 − 12 = ☐

18 $\frac{1}{2}$ of 18 = ☐

19 55 − 25 = ☐

20 36 + 26 =

21 70 ÷ 10 =

22 94 − 37 = ☐

23 $\frac{1}{3}$ of 9 = ☐

24. $\frac{3}{4}$ of 16 = ☐

25. ☐ + 28 = 64

END OF TEST

[Blank Page]

Key Stage One Mathematics

Set B
Paper 2: Reasoning

First name	
Middle name	
Last name	

For this test you are allowed to use:
a **pen** or a **pencil**   a **rubber**   and a **ruler**.

Total marks

1

[   ]

1 mark

2

[grapes]

1 mark

3

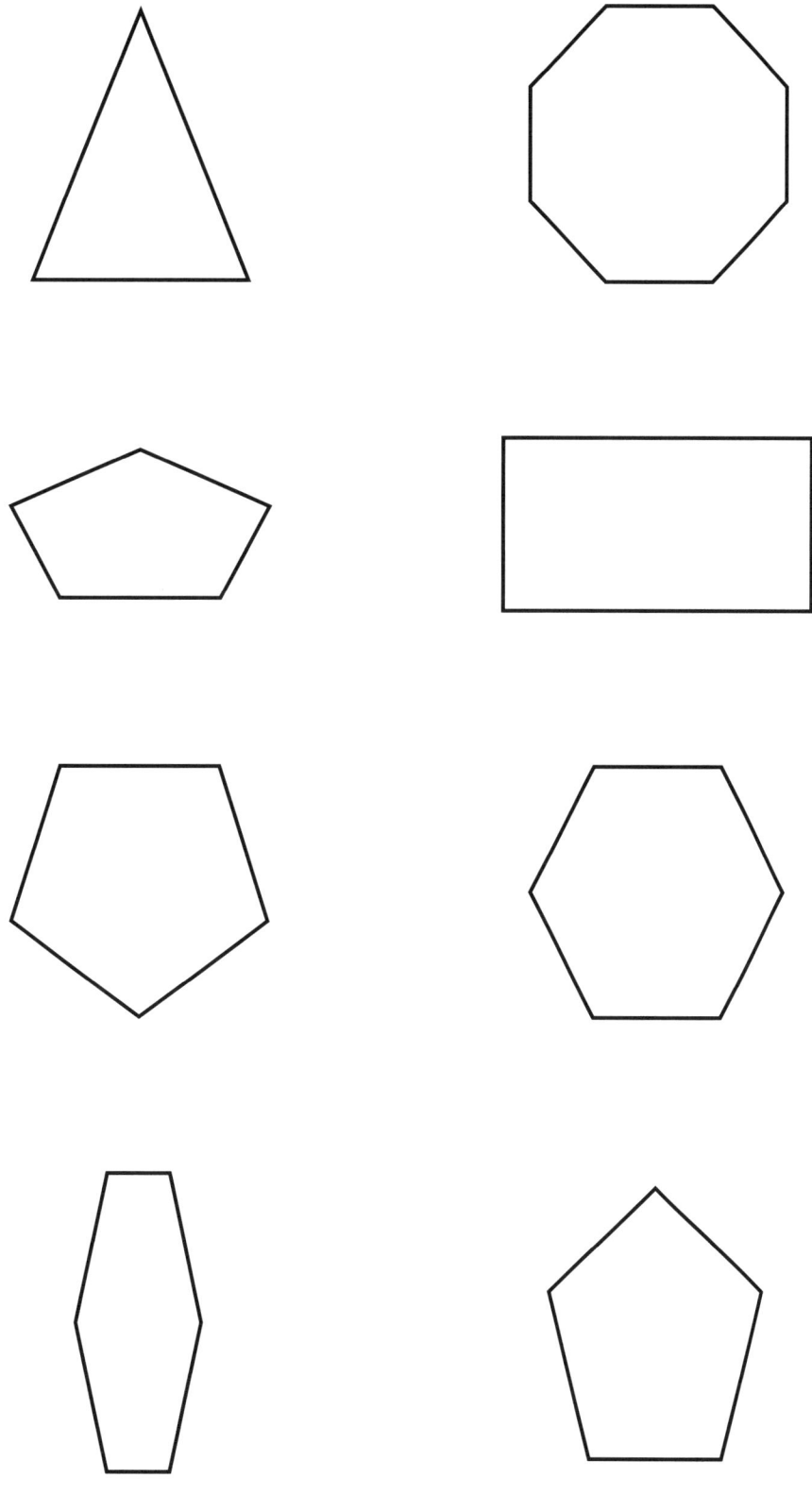

4

[_____ children]

1 mark

5

[_____ days]

1 mark

6 Put a cross (✗) next to the sentence that is false.

4 is half of 8. ☐

8 is half of 14. ☐

5 is half of 10. ☐

1 mark

7 Ruby has **96** paperclips.
Akil has one **more** paperclip than Ruby.

How many paperclips does Akil have?

paperclips

1 mark

8 Draw lines to match the numbers to the words.

sixteen   61

sixty-one   60

sixty   16

1 mark

9 Look at this number line.

The arrow is pointing to the number **38**.

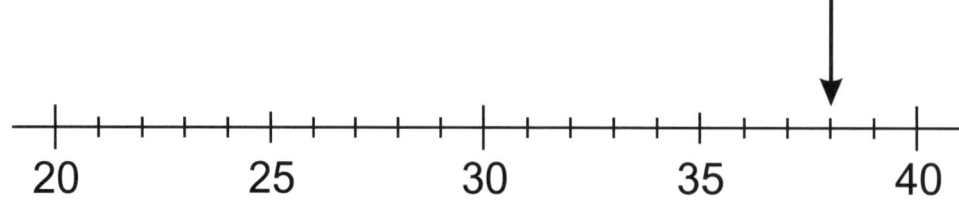

Find **10 less** than 38.
Draw an arrow on the number line to show your answer.

1 mark

10 Put a tick (✔) in the box under the glass that is **one quarter** full.

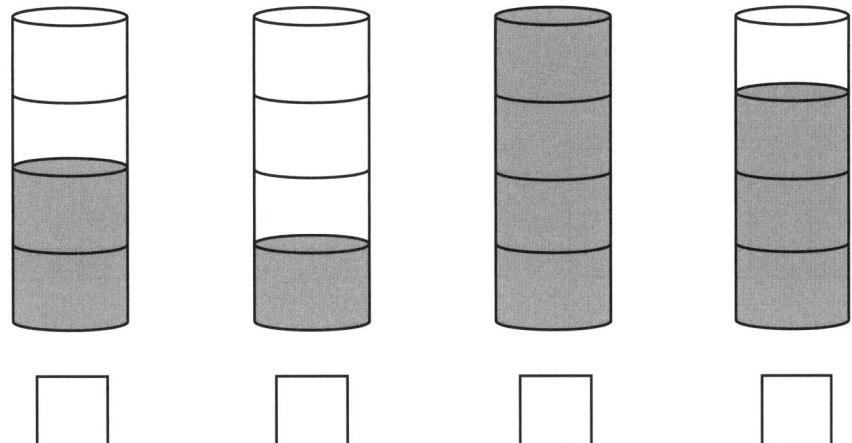

1 mark

11 Here are 4 symbols.

+ − × ÷

Fill in the boxes with the correct symbols.

33 = 16 ☐ 17

2 ☐ 6 = 12

1 mark

12 Put these numbers in order of size.
Start with the **smallest**.

71   47   74   45

☐   ☐   ☐   ☐

1 mark

13 Look at this 3D shape.

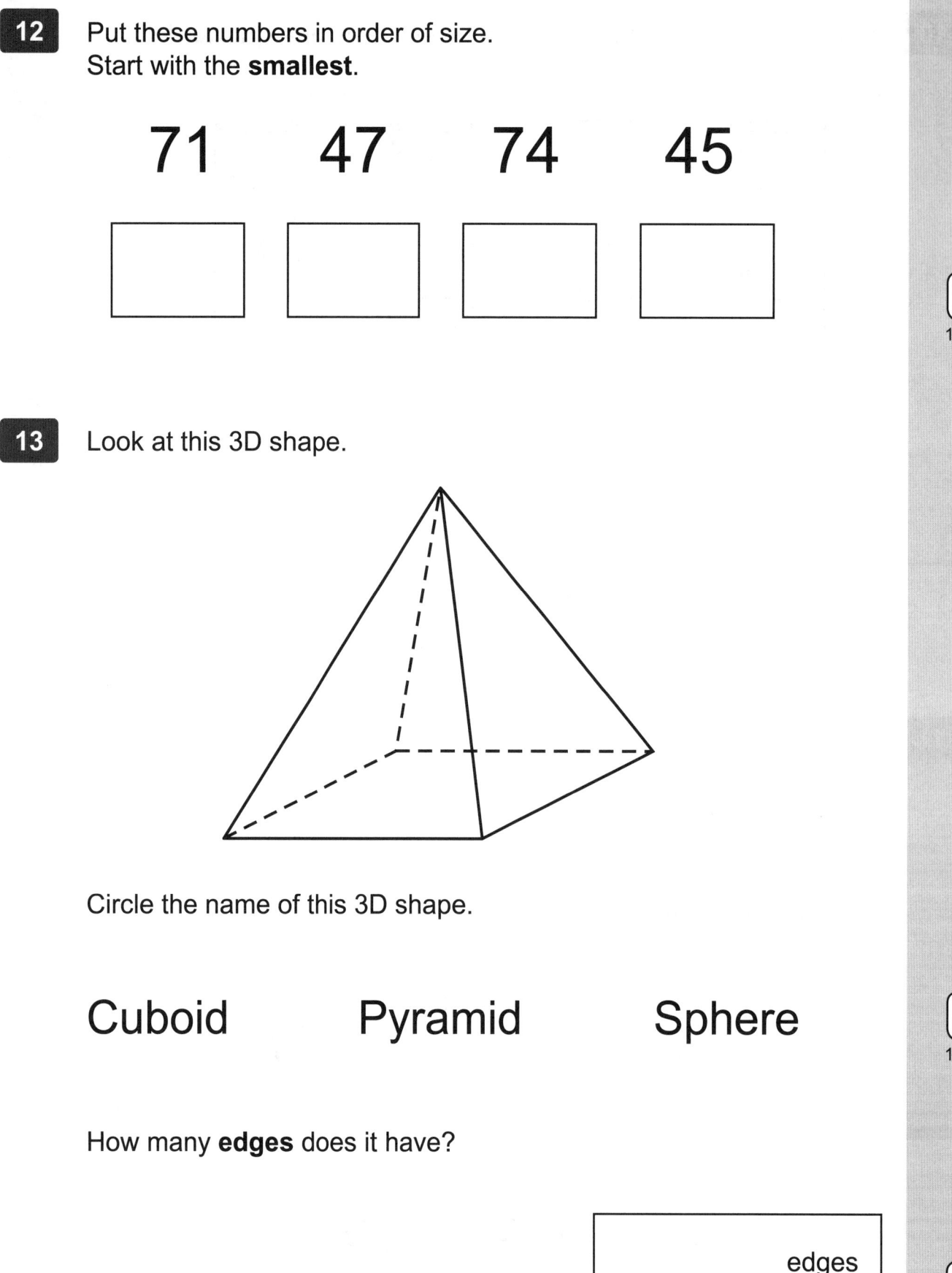

Circle the name of this 3D shape.

Cuboid   **Pyramid**   **Sphere**

1 mark

How many **edges** does it have?

☐ edges

1 mark

14 Akil works out 5 × 4.

Put a ring around the matching **sum**.

$$5 + 5 + 5 + 5 + 5$$

$$4 + 4 + 4 + 4 + 4$$

$$4 + 4 + 4 + 4$$

$$5 + 4 + 5 + 4$$

15 Draw hands on this clock to show the time '**half past nine**'.

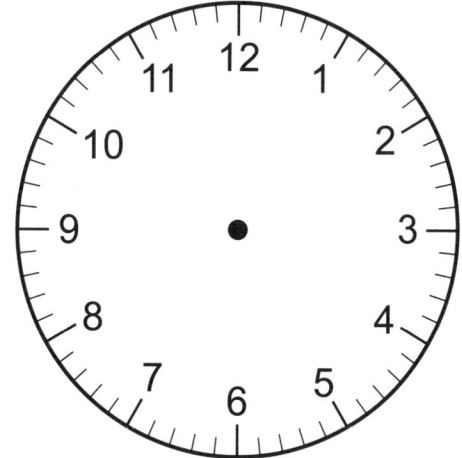

16 Fill in the boxes using the measurements below.

cm   kg   ml   °C

Ruby is 112 ☐ tall.

Akil's cat weighs 2 ☐ .

1 mark

17 Match the calculations that have the same answer.

5 × 4   19 + 4

7 + 16   2 × 10

9 + 9   9 × 2

1 mark

18 Chocolate bars come in packets of **5**.
Akil buys **8** packets of chocolate bars.

How many chocolate bars does Akil have in total?

chocolate bars

1 mark

19 This tally chart shows the favourite sports of children in Class 2.

Sport	Tally
Football	𝍷𝍷𝍷𝍷𝍷 𝍲
Hockey	
Netball	
Tennis	𝍺𝍺𝍺𝍺

3 children said 'Hockey' was their favourite
and **12** children said 'Netball' was their favourite.

Fill in the tally chart.

1 mark

20 Look at this sum.

$$63 + 37 = 100$$

Use this sum to fill in the missing numbers below.

$$100 - \boxed{} = 63$$

$$100 - \boxed{} = 37$$

1 mark

21 Ruby weighs a strawberry.

How much does the strawberry weigh?

g

1 mark

22 Look at this pattern.

△ □ ○ ○ △ □ ○ ○ △

Draw the next **two** shapes in this pattern.

1 mark

23 Put a ring around $\frac{3}{4}$ of these stars.

1 mark

24 Ruby has circled her birthday on this calendar.

May						
1	2	3	(4)	5	6	7
8	9	10	11	12	13	14
15	16	17	18	19	20	21
22	23	24	25	26	27	28
29	30	31				

The 1st of May is a Monday.

What **day** of the week is Ruby's birthday on?

Akil's birthday is in the month **before** Ruby's birthday.

What **month** is Akil's birthday in?

25 This graph shows the hair colours of some children.

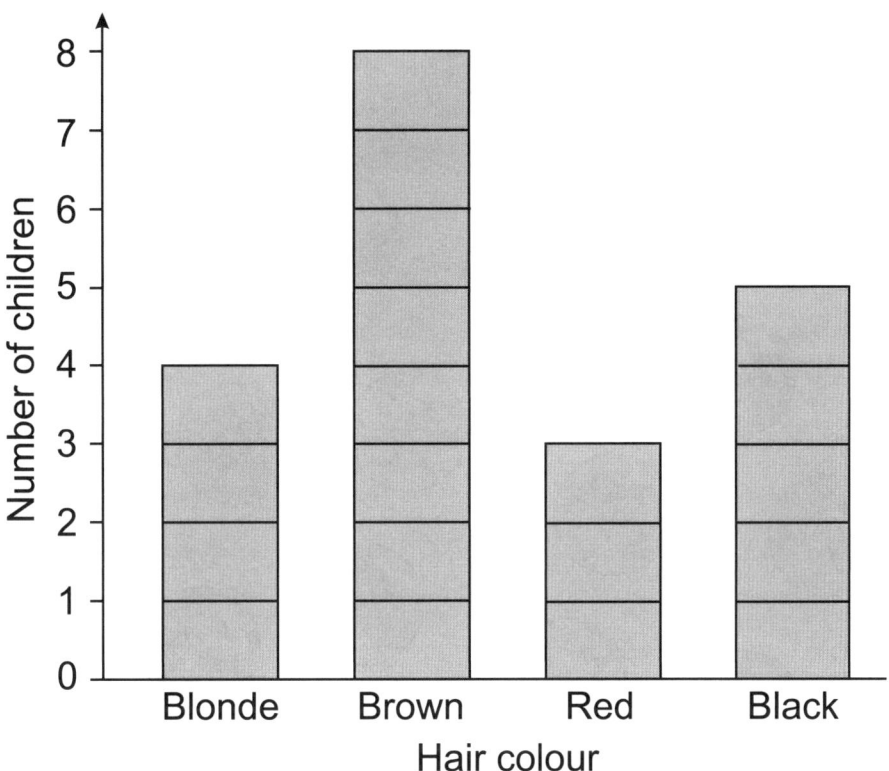

How many children were there **in total**?

children

1 mark

26 **64** children are going on a trip.

37 of these are going to the zoo.
The rest are going to the beach.

How many children are going to the beach?

children

1 mark

27 Here are Akil's marbles.

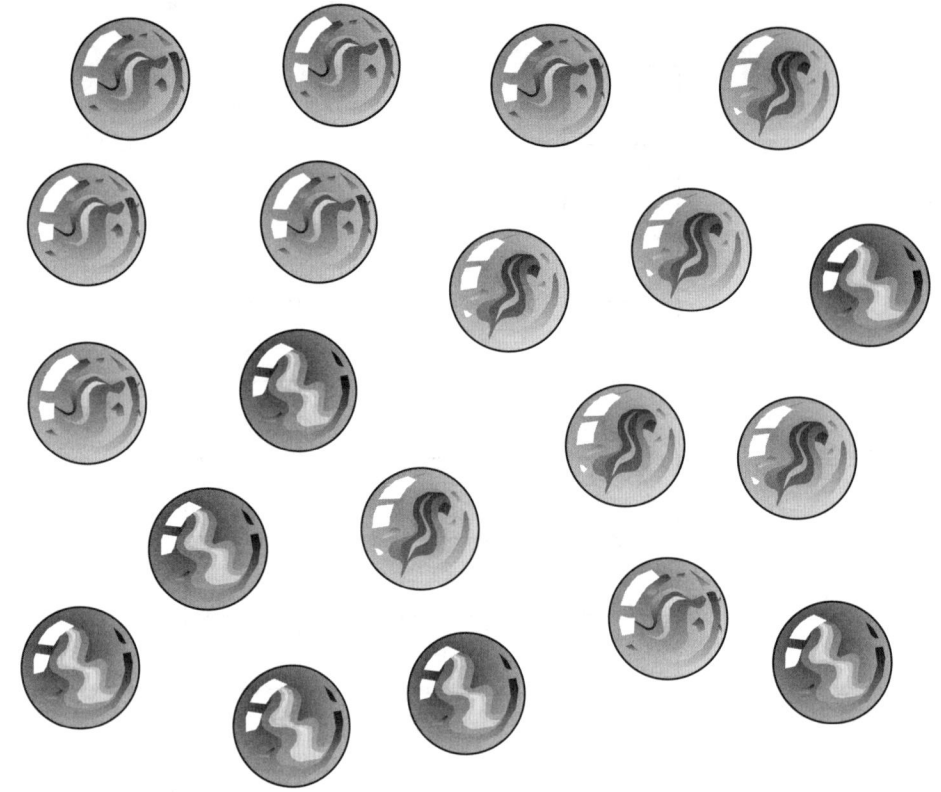

Akil sorts his marbles into **5** equal groups.
How many marbles are there in each group?

marbles

Ruby has **11** more marbles than Akil.
How many marbles does she have?

marbles

28 The numbers on this ladder go up by the same amount each time.

Fill in the missing numbers.

| 4 |
| |
| 24 |
| 34 |
| 44 |
| |
| |
| 74 |
| 84 |

1 mark

29 Ruby has **14** bananas.
Akil has **10** bananas.
They put all their bananas together then share them equally.

How many bananas do they each get?

Show your working.

bananas

30 Each week Akil gets **£4** pocket money.
He already has **£16** in his piggy bank.

Akil puts all his pocket money into the piggy bank.
How much money will there be in the piggy bank in 3 weeks' time?

Show your working.

£

2 marks

END OF TEST

[Blank Page]

CGP

Key Stage One
Mathematics
SATS Practice Papers

Instructions with Answers & Mark Scheme

Contents

Doing the Papers 3
Content Domain Coverage 5
Oral Questions 7
Answers 8

Practice is the best way to prepare for the KS1 Maths SATs...

...and this brilliant pack from CGP is bursting with the most realistic SATs practice you'll find, all fully up to date for the latest tests!

It contains two full sets of Practice Papers, each made up of two tests — just like the real Maths SATs pupils will take in Year 2.

We've also included full answers and mark schemes in this booklet. That means it's easy to find out which topics are their strongest, and what they need to concentrate on ahead of the SATs.

Published by CGP

Editors:
Chris Corrall, Shaun Harrogate, Caley Simpson, Ruth Wilbourne

Many thanks to Dawn Wright for proofreading.
Also thanks to Jan Greenway for the copyright research.

Coin images on Set A, Paper 2, pg 15 © iStock.com

Clipart from Corel®
Printed by Elanders Ltd, Newcastle upon Tyne.

Text, design, layout and original illustrations
© Coordination Group Publications Ltd. (CGP) 2017
All rights reserved.

National Curriculum references throughout reproduced under the terms of the Open Government Licence v3.0.
http://www.nationalarchives.gov.uk/doc/open-government-licence/version/3/

Photocopying more than 5% of this book is not permitted, even if you have a CLA licence.
Extra copies are available from CGP with next day delivery • 0800 1712 712 • www.cgpbooks.co.uk

Doing the Papers

There are **two sets** of practice papers in this pack — Set A and Set B.
Each set has **two papers** — Paper 1 and Paper 2.

Paper 1 is an **Arithmetic** test. It is worth **25 marks** and has 25 questions.

Paper 2 is a **Reasoning** test. It has **context** and **non-context** based questions.
It is worth **35 marks** and has about 30 questions.
The first **five** are oral questions — they're on page 7 of this booklet.
You have to read these questions out loud, making sure you
leave enough time for them to answer each question.
The **rest** of the questions are written in the paper.

Paper 1 should take about **20 minutes** and Paper 2 should take about
35 minutes (so around **55 minutes** in total). These aren't strict time limits,
so you can give them a bit of extra time to finish off if needed.

Make sure they have these things

A **pen** and a **pencil**.

A **ruler** that shows centimetres and millimetres.

A **rubber**.

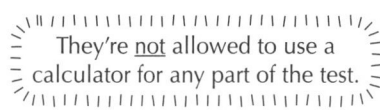
They're <u>not</u> allowed to use a calculator for any part of the test.

And remember...

1) Encourage them to write answers down **clearly**.
2) Tell them to read everything really **carefully** to be sure they're doing exactly what the question asks them to do.
3) If there are some questions they really can't do, they should **leave them out** and try the others.

KS1 Maths — Answers & Mark Scheme © CGP 2017

Keep a record of their scores

Mark their papers using the answers in this booklet, then **fill in** these tables.

	Set A		
	Paper 1	Paper 2	Total
Mark	/25	/35	/60

	Set B		
	Paper 1	Paper 2	Total
Mark	/25	/35	/60

The mark needed to achieve the **expected standard** varies from year to year, but if they get a total of **37** or more out of **60** on these papers then they should be on track.

Content Domain Coverage

The mark schemes in this Answer Book refer to the content domain references as they appear in the Standards & Testing Agency's 'Mathematics test framework' document.

Qu.	Requirement	Marks (Domain)
2	29	1 (2C1)

These refer to elements of the National Curriculum Programme of Study, which is split by Year.

For example, '2C1' refers to Year 2, substrand C1 ('add / subtract mentally').

You will see in the mark scheme that some substrands are divided further. For example, 'G1a' refers to 2-D shapes, while 'G1b' refers to 3-D shapes.

For a detailed breakdown on the content of each year's substrands, please visit the 'Mathematics test framework' document on the STA website.

Content Domain Coverage

This table sets out the areas of the content domain that are assessed in these papers.

Topic	Sub-strand	Ref	Set A		Set B	
			Paper 1	Paper 2	Paper 1	Paper 2
Number and place value	counting (in multiples)	N1	Q5, 12	Q2, 18	Q3	Q1, 28
	read, write, order and compare numbers	N2		Q1, 23		Q8, 12
	identify, represent and rounding	N4		Q12		Q9
	number problems	N6			Q16	
Addition, subtraction, multiplication and division (calculations)	add / subtract mentally	C1	Q9	Q10	Q2, 9, 16	Q1
	add / subtract using written methods	C2	Q1, 2, 3, 7, 14, 15, 17, 21, 22		Q1, 5, 7, 10, 12, 14, 17, 19, 20, 22, 25	
	use inverses and check	C3	Q9		Q12, 25	Q20
	add / subtract to solve problems	C4	Q4, 24	Q2, 7, 11, 13, 20, 28	Q6	Q2, 7, 11, 17, 26, 27, 29
	multiply / divide mentally	C6	Q6, 8, 10, 11, 13, 18, 19, 23	Q4	Q4, 8, 11, 13, 15, 21	Q4, 5, 17, 18
	multiply / divide using written methods	C7				
	solve problems based on all four operations and knowledge of the commutative facts	C8		Q14, 27, 30		Q14, 27, 29, 30
	order of operations	C9		Q25		
Fractions	recognise, find, write, name and count fractions	F1	Q16, 20, 25	Q5, 19, 22	Q18, 23, 24	Q6, 10, 23
	equivalent fractions	F2				
Measurement	compare, describe and order measures	M1		Q6		
	measure and read scales	M2		Q16		Q16, 21
	money	M3				
	telling time, ordering time and units of time	M4		Q21, 26		Q15, 24
	solve mathematical problems involving measures	M9		Q24, 28		Q30

KS1 Maths — Answers & Mark Scheme

Content Domain Coverage

Topic	Sub-strand	Ref	Set A		Set B	
			Paper 1	Paper 2	Paper 1	Paper 2
Geometry — properties of shape	recognise and name common shapes	G1		Q3, 8		Q3, 13
	describe properties and classify shapes	G2		Q9, 15		Q13
	draw and make shapes and relate 2-D to 3-D shapes	G3				
Geometry — position and direction	patterns	P1				Q22
	describe position, direction and movement	P2		Q29		
Statistics	interpret and represent data	S1		Q17		Q19
	solve problems involving data	S2				Q25

Oral Questions

Set A Practice Paper 2

1. Write the number 'one hundred and twelve'.

2. Poppy is thinking of a number. It is 3 more than 12.
   Write the number Poppy is thinking of.

3. Look at the shapes on page 3. Put a cross on all the shapes that are cuboids.

4. Daniel has 4 cards that show the numbers 5, 13, 18 and 21.
   Which number is even?

5. Daniel has 16 oranges. He gives away half of the oranges.
   How many oranges does he have left?

Set B Practice Paper 2

1. What number is 6 less than 20?

2. Ruby has 26 grapes. Akil has 10 more grapes than Ruby.
   How many grapes does Akil have?

3. Look at the shapes on page 3. Put a tick inside all the pentagons.

4. 15 children are divided into 5 equal teams.
   How many children are there in each team?

5. How many days are there in 5 weeks?

Set A — Answers

Practice Paper 1 — Arithmetic

Qu.	Requirement	Marks (Domain)
1	13	1 (1C2a)
2	11	1 (1C2a)
3	19	1 (1C2a)
4	12	1 (1C4)
5	35	1 (2N1)
6	12	1 (2C6)
7	11	1 (2C2b)
8	20	1 (2C6)
9	60	1 (2C1/2C3)
10	20	1 (2C6)
11	8	1 (2C6)
12	58	1 (2N1)
13	6	1 (2C6)
14	7	1 (2C2b)
15	39	1 (2C2b)
16	7	1 (1F1a/2F1a)
17	60	1 (2C2b)
18	100	1 (2C6)
19	15	1 (2C6)
20	4	1 (2F1a)
21	73	1 (2C2b)
22	25	1 (2C2b)
23	12	1 (2C6)
24	35	1 (2C4)
25	9	1 (2F1a)

Practice Paper 2 — Reasoning

Qu.	Requirement	Marks (Domain)
1	112	1 (2N2a)
2	15	1 (1C4/2N1)
3	(X on rectangular prism, X on small cuboid, X on cube)	1 (1G1b)
4	18	1 (2C6)
5	8 oranges	1 (1F1a/2F1a)
6	(armchair circled)	1 (1M1)
7	− +	1 (1C4)
8	Hexagon	1 (1G1a/2G1a)
9	6 faces	1 (2G2b)
10	Any one of: 70, 20 and 10 60, 30 and 10 50, 40 and 10 50, 30 and 20	1 (2C1)
11	25 ice creams	1 (2C4)
12	Accept either 66 or 67.	1 (2N4)
13	14 toy cars	1 (2C4)
14	40 chocolate buttons 5 boxes (1 mark for each correct answer)	2 (2C8)

KS1 Maths — Answers & Mark Scheme © CGP 2017

Set A — Answers

Qu.	Requirement	Marks (Domain)
15	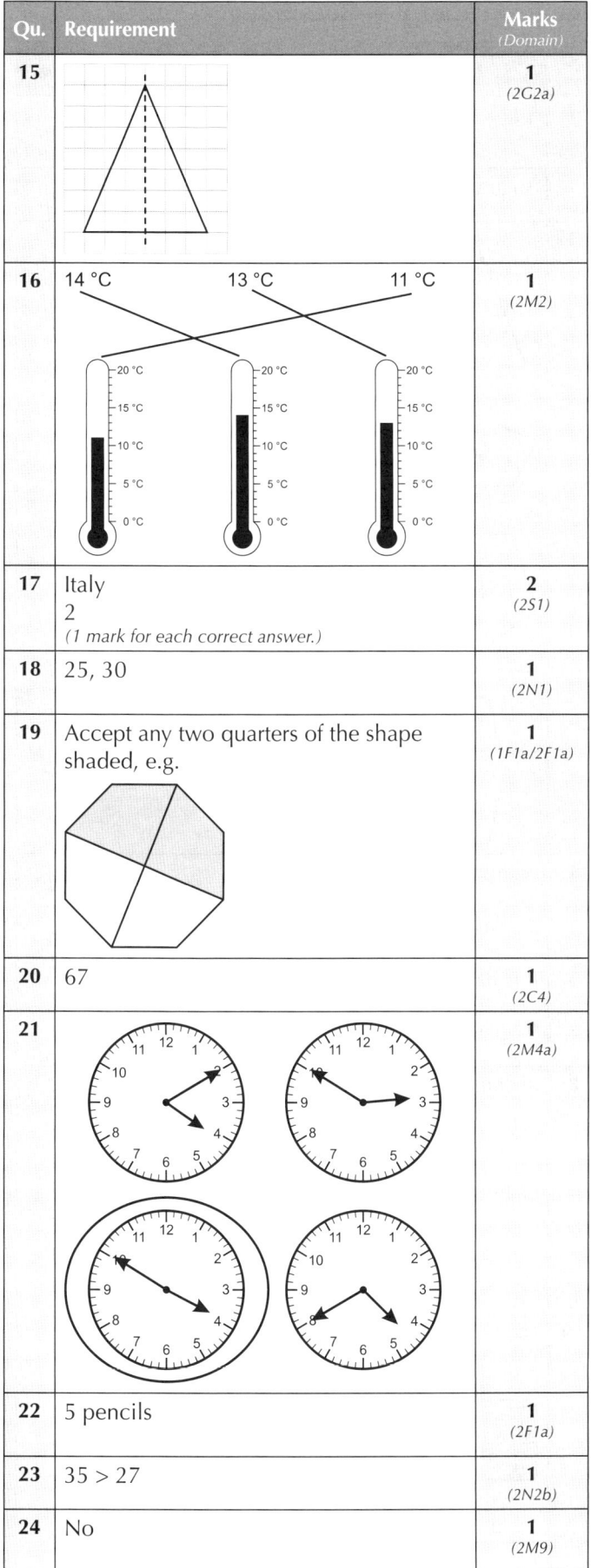	1 (2G2a)
16	14 °C — 13 °C — 11 °C (lines crossing to thermometers)	1 (2M2)
17	Italy 2 (1 mark for each correct answer.)	2 (2S1)
18	25, 30	1 (2N1)
19	Accept any two quarters of the shape shaded, e.g.	1 (1F1a/2F1a)
20	67	1 (2C4)
21	(clocks)	1 (2M4a)
22	5 pencils	1 (2F1a)
23	35 > 27	1 (2N2b)
24	No	1 (2M9)

Qu.	Requirement	Marks (Domain)
25	(4 + 7) 4 − 8 8 − 4 (7 + 4) 3 ÷ 9 (3 × 6) 9 ÷ 3 (6 × 3) (1 mark for each correct pair.)	2 (2C9a/2C9b)
26	after	1 (1M4b)
27	9 days	1 (2C8)
28	£38 (2 marks for correct answer, otherwise 1 mark for a correct method)	2 (2C4/2M9)
29	(tick on correct pattern)	1 (1P2)
30	Yes (2 marks for correct answer, otherwise 1 mark for a correct method.)	2 (2C8)

Set B — Answers

Practice Paper 1 — Arithmetic

Qu.	Requirement	Marks (Domain)
1	2	1 (1C2a)
2	29	1 (2C1)
3	47	1 (1N1b)
4	14	1 (2C6)
5	42	1 (2C2b)
6	3	1 (1C4)
7	38	1 (2C2b)
8	40	1 (2C6)
9	17	1 (2C1)
10	21	1 (2C2b)
11	9	1 (2C6)
12	80	1 (2C3/2C2b)
13	35	1 (2C6)
14	47	1 (2C2b)
15	10	1 (2C6)
16	80	1 (2N6/2C1)
17	25	1 (2C2b)
18	9	1 (1F1a/2F1a)
19	30	1 (2C2b)
20	62	1 (2C2b)
21	7	1 (2C6)
22	57	1 (2C2b)
23	3	1 (2F1a)
24	12	1 (2F1a)
25	36	1 (2C2b/2C3)

Practice Paper 2 — Reasoning

Qu.	Requirement	Marks (Domain)
1	14	1 (2N1/1C2a)
2	36 grapes	1 (2C4)
3	Ticks on pentagon, pentagon, and pentagon	1 (1G1a/2G1a)
4	3 children	1 (2C6)
5	35 days	1 (2C6)
6	8 is half of 14.	1 (1F1a)
7	97 paperclips	1 (1C4)
8	sixteen — 16, sixty-one — 61, sixty — 60	1 (1N2a/2N2a)
9	Arrows at 28 and 38 on number line	1 (2N4)
10	Tick on second cylinder	1 (1F1b)
11	+, ×	1 (1C4)
12	45, 47, 71, 74	1 (2N2b)

KS1 Maths — Answers & Mark Scheme © CGP 2017

Set B — Answers

Qu.	Requirement	Marks (Domain)
13	Pyramid 8 edges *(1 mark for each correct answer.)*	2 (1G1b/2G2b)
14	5 + 5 + 5 + 5 + 5 **(4 + 4 + 4 + 4 + 4)** ← circled 4 + 4 + 4 + 4 5 + 4 + 5 + 4	1 (2C8)
15	Clock showing hands at 9 and 5 (9:25)	1 (1M4a)
16	cm kg	1 (2M2)
17	5 × 4 — 19 + 4 7 + 16 — 2 × 10 9 + 9 — 9 × 2	1 (2C4/2C6)
18	40 chocolate bars	1 (2C6)
19	Tally table: Football |||| ||, Hockey |||, Netball |||| |||| ||, Tennis ||||	1 (2S1)
20	37 63	1 (2C3)
21	27 g	1 (2M2)
22	□ ○	1 (2P1)

Qu.	Requirement	Marks (Domain)
23	Accept a ring around any nine stars, e.g.	1 (2F1a)
24	Thursday April *(1 mark for each correct answer.)*	2 (1M4c)
25	20 children	1 (2S2b)
26	27 children	1 (2C4)
27	4 marbles 31 marbles	2 (2C4/2C8)
28	14 54 64	1 (2N1)
29	12 bananas *(2 marks for correct answer, otherwise 1 mark for a correct method)*	2 (2C4/2C8)
30	£28 *(2 marks for correct answer, otherwise 1 mark for a correct method)*	2 (2C8/2M9)

CGP

MHEP13U

www.cgpbooks.co.uk